In the Footsteps of Our Ancestors

In the Footsteps of Our Ancestors

Linda Standridge

Published by Linda Standridge, 2023.

While every precaution has been taken in the preparation of this book, the publisher assumes no responsibility for errors or omissions, or for damages resulting from the use of the information contained herein.

IN THE FOOTSTEPS OF OUR ANCESTORS

First edition. December 15, 2023.

ISBN: 979-8223672975

Written by Linda Standridge.

Table of Contents

Linda Standridge

A Journey through Prehistory and Ancient Civilizations

Chapter One:

The Dawn of Prehistoric Civilizations

The Origins of Humanity:

In the vast expanse of time, stretching back millions of years, lies the intriguing story of our origins as a species - Homo sapiens. We will explore the remarkable journey of prehistoric civilizations and societies, from the earliest traces of our ancestors to the emergence of Homo sapiens.

Deep within the mists of time, our ancestors began to take their first tentative steps towards humanity. The journey begins with Australopithecus, who inhabited the African continent around 4 million years ago. These early hominins were bipedal, walking on two legs, and showed the first signs of tool use. As the climate changed, our ancestors adapted and evolved, giving rise to new species such as Homo habilis and Homo erectus.

The story of humanity takes a significant turn with the emergence of Homo sapiens, our direct ancestors, around 300,000 years ago. With their larger brains and advanced cognitive abilities, Homo sapiens exhibited a remarkable capacity for innovation and creativity. They crafted sophisticated tools, developed complex social structures, and even created symbolic art. This marked the beginning of a new era in human history.

To understand our origins we must also explore the migrations of early humans. Around 70,000 years ago, Homo sapiens began to venture beyond Africa, gradually populating other parts of the world. The fossil record and genetic studies have revealed that our ancestors encountered other hominin species, such as Neanderthals and Denisovans, and interbred with them. These encounters shaped our genetic diversity and enriched our collective heritage.

From the earliest cave paintings in Europe to elaborate burial rituals in ancient Mesopotamia, these early societies laid the groundwork for the complex civilizations to follow. The development of agriculture, the establishment of permanent settlements, and the emergence of symbolic language played pivotal roles in shaping human societies.

The Origins of Humanity is a captivating tale of resilience, adaptation, and ingenuity. By understanding our roots, we gain a deeper appreciation for the legacy they have left behind and the profound impact they had on shaping the world we inhabit today. We will embark on a journey through time, tracing the footsteps of our ancestors from hunter-gatherers to civilizations.

The Paleolithic Era: Hunters and Gatherers

In the vast expanse of human history, the Paleolithic Era holds a special place when our ancestors first stepped on the path of civilization. It is a period that witnessed the emergence of Homo sapiens, our species, and the remarkable advancements in our abilities to survive, adapt, and thrive. Join us as we delve into the captivating world of the Paleolithic Era, exploring the lives of our hunter-gatherer ancestors.

During this epoch, which spanned from approximately 2.6 million to 10,000 years ago, Homo sapiens honed their survival skills as hunters and gatherers. With a deep understanding of their natural surroundings, they navigated the diverse landscapes that characterized the era, from dense forests to expansive grasslands. Armed with an intimate knowledge of the flora and fauna, they skillfully hunted animals for food, clothing, and tools. Equally important was their expertise in gathering edible plants, nuts, and berries, ensuring a varied and nutritious diet.

The Paleolithic Era was marked by the use of stone tools, which revolutionized the way our ancestors interacted with their environment. These tools, crafted through a meticulous process of flaking and shaping stones, enabled them to butcher animals, skin hides, and fashion weaponry for hunting. Beyond their practical uses, these tools also played a crucial role in social interactions, symbolizing the development of complex communication and trade networks.

The nomadic lifestyle was a defining characteristic of Paleolithic societies. Our ancestors were constantly on the move, following the migration patterns of animals and the seasonal abundance of resources. This mobility allowed them to adapt to changing environments and expand their territories. It also fostered a strong sense of communal living, as groups of individuals worked together to ensure survival and protect each other from potential threats.

While the Paleolithic Era has often been romanticized as a simpler time, it was far from idyllic. Our ancestors faced numerous challenges, including harsh climates, encounters with large predators, and the constant search for food and water. Yet, their ability to overcome these obstacles and develop sophisticated strategies for survival laid the foundation for future civilizations.

By studying the Paleolithic Era, we gain invaluable insights into our shared history and the remarkable achievements of our early ancestors. Their ingenuity, adaptability, and cooperative nature paved the way for the development of complex societies in the millennia that followed.

The Neolithic Revolution: From Nomads to Settled Communities.

In the vast annals of human history, one epoch stands out as a pivotal turning point that forever altered the course of civilization – the Neolithic Revolution—this momentous period marked the shift from a nomadic way of life to settled communities, laying the foundation for the complex societies we inhabit today. We will explore the fascinating journey of our ancestors as they transitioned from hunters and gatherers to farmers and builders, reshaping the very fabric of human existence.

The Neolithic Revolution emerged approximately 10,000 years ago, showcasing extraordinary transformations in human behavior, technological advancements, and social structures. Before this revolution, our ancestors roamed the Earth in small groups, constantly in search of food and shelter. But as they began to understand the secrets of agriculture, everything changed. No longer dependent on the unpredictable whims of nature, early humans learned to cultivate crops and domesticate animals. This newfound ability to produce their own food brought about a radical shift in their lifestyle, allowing them to establish permanent settlements.

As we trace the footsteps of our ancestors through this pivotal era, we will encounter the birth of agriculture and witness the rise of the first farming communities. From the fertile lands of Mesopotamia to the Nile Valley in Egypt we will explore the various regions where this revolution took hold. We will delve into the methods of early farming, the cultivation of essential crops such as wheat and barley, and the domestication of animals like goats and sheep.

But the Neolithic Revolution was not merely about food production; it also sparked profound social changes. With the establishment of settled communities, humans developed specialized skills, leading to the emergence of artisans, craftsmen, and traders. The surplus food produced by agriculture allowed for population growth, leading to the development of complex social hierarchies and the birth of organized religion.

The Neolithic Revolution marked a pivotal transition in human history, transforming our ancestors from nomadic hunters and gatherers into settled communities. Join us as we journey through the captivating world of our prehistoric civilizations, shedding light on the remarkable developments that laid the groundwork for uncovering the secrets of the Neolithic Revolution and paying homage to the remarkable achievements of our ancestors.

Gobekli Tepe near Sanlurfa Turkey

KARAHAN TEPE, TURKEY

Derinkuyu in Cappadocia

Chapter Two:

Ancient Mesopotamia: Cradle of Civilization

The Sumerians: City-States and Ziggurats

The Sumerians, one of the earliest known civilizations in human history, left a lasting legacy in the form of advanced city-states and majestic ziggurats. These ancient people flourished in the region of Mesopotamia, which is modern-day Iraq, between the Tigris and Euphrates rivers. Their contributions to prehistoric civilizations and societies are remarkable and continue to captivate historians and archeologists alike.

The Sumerians were pioneers of urbanization, establishing some of the world's first cities around 4000 BCE. These city-states were centers of political, economic, and cultural life. Each city-state was an independent entity, with its own government, laws, and religious practices. Prominent among these city-states were Uruk, Ur, and Lagash. The Sumerians developed a complex administrative system to govern their cities, paving the way for future civilizations.

One of the most iconic architectural achievements of the Sumerians was the construction of ziggurats. These monumental stepped structures served as temples to honor their gods. Ziggurats were made of mud bricks and rose several stories high, often dominating the city skyline. The most famous ziggurat was the Temple of Marduk in Babylon, which stood as a symbol of the city's power and religious devotion. Ziggurats were not only places of worship but also served as administrative centers and repositories for cultural and historical artifacts.

The Sumerians' religious beliefs played a crucial role in shaping their society. They worshiped a pantheon of deities, each associated with various aspects of life, such as agriculture, warfare, and fertility. The Sumerians believed that their gods controlled the forces of nature and, in turn, sought their favor through elaborate rituals and sacrifices.

The ziggurats were seen as a physical connection between the earthly and divine realms, serving as a conduit for communication with the gods.

Trade was a vital component of Sumerian society. The Sumerians developed an extensive network of trade routes, connecting them to neighboring regions and beyond. They traded various commodities, including agricultural products, textiles, pottery, and precious metals. This economic prosperity allowed the Sumerians to develop a sophisticated society with specialized professions, including scribes, craftsmen, and merchants.

The Sumerians also made significant advancements in writing, known as cuneiform. This system of wedge-shaped marks on clay tablets revolutionized communication and record-keeping. It enabled the preservation of laws, literature, and historical accounts, and ensured the Sumerian legacy would endure.

The Sumerians' achievements in city-state governance, ziggurat construction, religious practices, trade, and writing laid the foundation for future civilizations. Their legacy as pioneers of urbanization, advanced architecture, and cultural development continues to fascinate and inspire us today. By studying the Sumerians, we gain valuable insight into the origins of prehistoric civilizations and societies, appreciating the achievements of our ancestors.

The Akkadians and Babylonians: Hammurabi's Code

In the mesmerizing tapestry of prehistoric civilizations, the Akkadians and Babylonians shine as beacons of ancient wisdom and innovation. Their contributions to the development of early societies are immeasurable, but perhaps none is more significant than Hammurabi's Code, a remarkable legal system that laid the foundation for modern justice.

The Akkadians, under the reign of their great leader Sargon of Akkad, established the first empire in history around 2300 BCE. This empire encompassed vast territories and diverse cultures, with Sargon promoting unity through a centralized government. However, it was Hammurabi, the sixth king of the Babylonian Empire, who left an indelible mark on the annals of history.

Hammurabi ascended to the throne in 1792 BCE and embarked on a mission to establish a just and orderly society. His code, engraved on a stele of black diorite, contained 282 laws that governed every aspect of life in Babylon. These laws were not only revolutionary but also a reflection of the societal norms and values of the time.

The Code of Hammurabi emphasized the principles of retribution and the concept of "an eye for an eye." It aimed to maintain social order by providing clear guidelines for behavior and punishment. The laws covered a wide range of subjects, from family matters and property rights to trade regulations and labor contracts.

One of the distinguishing features of Hammurabi's Code was its focus on social hierarchy. The penalties for offenses varied depending on the perpetrator's social status, with severe punishments reserved for lower classes. This hierarchy reflected the existing power dynamics and entrenched the privileges of the ruling elite.

Despite its flaws, Hammurabi's Code had a profound impact on the development of legal systems around the world. It established the concept of legal equality, as it applied to both the rich and the poor. Furthermore, it emphasized the idea that a ruler's duty was to ensure justice and protect the weak. These principles would shape the legal systems of future civilizations, acting as a precursor to the modern rule of law.

The Akkadians and Babylonians, with their rich cultural heritage and groundbreaking legal system, provide a glimpse into the origins of prehistoric civilizations. Hammurabi's Code stands as a testament to the ingenuity and societal complexities of these ancient civilizations, leaving a lasting legacy that continues to shape our understanding of justice and governance.

The Assyrians and Chaldeans: Empires of the Fertile Crescent

In the vast expanse of the Fertile Crescent, nestled between the Tigris and Euphrates rivers, emerged two mighty empires that would leave an indelible mark on the annals of prehistoric civilizations: The Assyrians and Chaldeans. We will delve into their rise, achievements, and eventual decline, shedding light on the fascinating world of ancient Mesopotamia.

The Assyrian Empire, which reached its zenith in the 8th and 7th centuries BCE, was characterized by its formidable military prowess and ruthless conquests. With a highly organized army and advanced siege warfare techniques, the Assyrians swiftly expanded their empire and subjugated vast territories from Egypt to Persia. Their capital, Nineveh, stood as a testament to their architectural ingenuity, boasting grand palaces adorned with intricate reliefs and the famous Hanging Gardens.

While the Assyrians were known for their military might, the Chaldeans ascended to power through their mastery of astronomy and astrology. Under the leadership of King Nabopolassar, the Chaldeans overthrew the Assyrian Empire and established the Neo-Babylonian Empire. Their capital, Babylon, was a canter of learning and culture, with the iconic Hanging Gardens considered one of the Seven Wonders of the Ancient World.

However, the Assyrians and Chaldeans were not just conquerors and builders; they were also pioneers in various fields. The Assyrians developed a sophisticated system of governance, with an extensive bureaucracy ensuring efficient administration. They also fostered a vibrant intellectual culture, preserving and translating the works of earlier civilizations, such as the Code of Hammurabi. The Chaldeans, on the other hand, made significant contributions to mathematics and astronomy, using their observations of celestial bodies to create accurate calendars and predict celestial events.

Despite their achievements, both empires eventually succumbed to internal strife and external invasions. The Assyrians and Chaldeans endure to this day, with their advancements in warfare, governance, and intellectual pursuits shaping the course of history. By studying their civilization, we gain valuable insights into the complexities of prehistoric societies and the foundations upon which the modern world is built.

Trade and Interaction: Connections with Mesopotamia and Egypt

Throughout history, trade and interaction between civilizations have played a crucial role in shaping the development and progress of societies. In the prehistoric era, two great civilizations emerged in the regions of Mesopotamia and Egypt. These civilizations not only laid the foundation for future advanced societies but also established a network of trade and interaction that spanned vast distances.

Mesopotamia, often referred to as the "Cradle of Civilization," was situated between the Tigris and Euphrates Rivers. This fertile land provided the perfect environment for agricultural practices, leading to the rise of city-states such as Ur, Uruk, and Babylon. With a surplus of food, these early Mesopotamian societies sought to expand their influence and establish trade routes with neighboring regions.

One of the most significant trade partners for Mesopotamia was Egypt, located to the west. Egypt, known as the "Gift of the Nile," relied heavily on the Nile River for its agricultural prosperity. The surplus of crops, such as wheat, barley, and flax, allowed the Egyptians to engage in extensive trade with their Mesopotamian counterparts.

The trade between Mesopotamia and Egypt was not limited to agricultural products alone. These civilizations exchanged various goods, including precious metals like gold and silver, gemstones, timber, textiles, and even livestock. This vibrant trade network not only benefited the economies of both regions but also fostered cultural exchange and the spread of ideas.

The trade routes connecting Mesopotamia and Egypt were not without challenges. The vast distances and geographical obstacles required the development of efficient transportation methods.

Caravans of pack animals, including donkeys and camels, were employed to transport goods across deserts and rugged terrains.

Moreover, the trade between these civilizations was not solely limited to physical goods. Ideas, technologies, and cultural practices were also exchanged, enriching the societies of both Mesopotamia and Egypt. The development of writing systems, for instance, was influenced by the exchange of ideas between these civilizations, leading to the rise of cuneiform script in Mesopotamia and hieroglyphics in Egypt.

The trade and interaction between Mesopotamia and Egypt played a pivotal role in the development of prehistoric civilizations. Through the exchange of goods, ideas, and cultural practices, these civilizations not only thrived economically but also embraced diversity and innovation. The trade routes connecting these regions served as a bridge, fostering connections that would shape the course of future civilizations. Understanding the significance of these trade networks allows us to appreciate the rich tapestry of prehistoric societies and their contributions to human history.

Mesopotamian Civilization

MESOPOTAMIAN CYLINDER seals

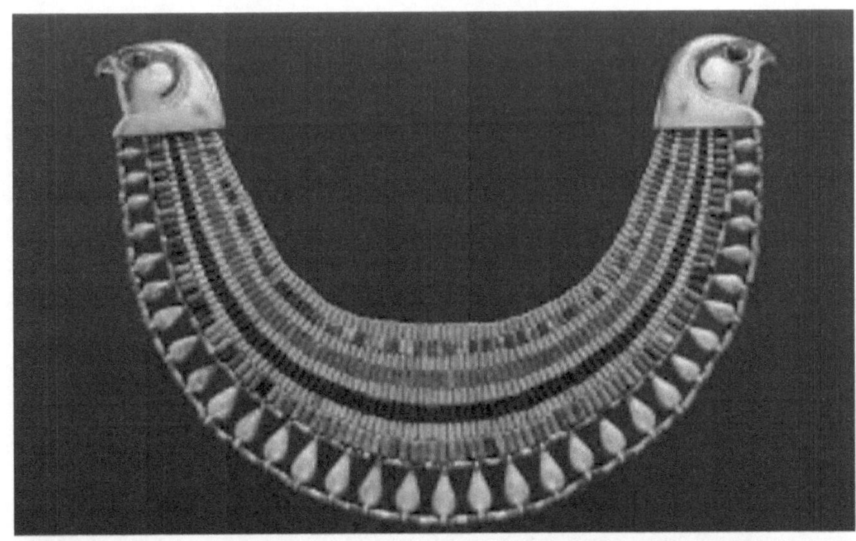

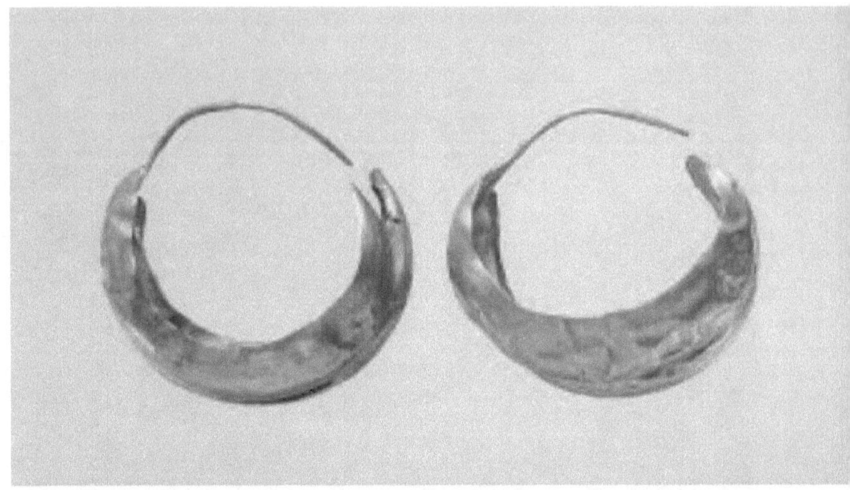

ISHTAR GATE

Sumerian city

Cuneiform tablets from Mesopotamia

Chapter Three:

Ancient Egypt: Land of the Pharaohs and Pyramids

The Nile River: Lifeblood of the Egyptians

In the realm of prehistoric civilizations and societies, few have left an indelible mark on history like the ancient Egyptians. At the heart of their thriving civilization lay a majestic river that shaped their culture, sustenance, and ultimately their destiny - the Nile River. It is often said that the Nile was the lifeblood that flowed through the veins of ancient Egypt, providing the essential nourishment needed to sustain their flourishing society.

The Nile River, the longest river in the world, stretches over 4,000 miles, traversing eleven modern-day countries. However, it is in Egypt where this mighty river takes on an unparalleled significance. The annual flooding of the Nile, known as the inundation, was the cornerstone of Egyptian life. Every year, when the waters swelled and overflowed onto the surrounding floodplains, they brought with them rich silt, rejuvenating the soil and creating fertile land for agriculture. This natural phenomenon allowed the Egyptians to cultivate crops and sustain a bountiful harvest, ensuring their survival.

The Nile not only provided sustenance, but it also served as the primary transportation route for the ancient Egyptians. The river acted as a bustling highway where boats, barges, and rafts were used to transport goods, people, and ideas. The Egyptians skillfully navigated the Nile, connecting different regions of their civilization and facilitating the exchange of goods and knowledge. This interconnectivity played a pivotal role in the development of their society, allowing for the growth of trade, the sharing of ideas, and the spread of cultural practices.

Beyond its practical importance, the Nile held a profound spiritual significance for the Egyptians. They believed that the river was a gift from the gods, a divine entity that sustained their existence. The Nile was personified as the god Hapy, revered and worshiped for its life-giving waters. The annual inundation was seen as a manifestation of the god's benevolence, and the Egyptians held elaborate festivals and ceremonies to honor and appease the river deities.

The importance of the Nile in ancient Egyptian society cannot be overstated. It was the foundation upon which their civilization flourished, providing sustenance, transportation, and spiritual nourishment. The river brought prosperity, abundance, and cultural exchange to the ancient Egyptians, allowing them to build one of the most enduring and influential civilizations in history.

As we journey through the footprints of our ancestors, we cannot help but marvel at the significance of the Nile River. It is a testament to the ingenuity and resourcefulness of prehistoric civilizations, and a reminder of the profound impact that natural elements can have on shaping human history. The story of the Nile is a captivating tale of the symbiotic relationship between humans and their environment, showcasing the remarkable achievements and resilience of our ancient forebears.

Welcome to the enchanting world of the Old Kingdom! We will delve into the captivating era of ancient Egypt, where mighty pharaohs ruled with divine authority and colossal pyramids rose towards the heavens. Join us on a journey through time as we explore the fascinating civilization that flourished along the banks of the Nile.

The Old Kingdom, also known as the Age of the Pyramids, spanned from approximately 2686 to 2181 BCE. It was a period characterized by powerful pharaohs who consolidated their authority over the land and embraced a divine status. These god-kings were revered as the earthly embodiments of the gods Horus and Ra, responsible for maintaining ma'at, the eternal order of the universe.

But what truly captured the imagination of the world and continues to astonish us today is the monumental pyramid-building endeavor undertaken by the pharaohs. These awe-inspiring structures, such as the Great Pyramid of Giza, stand as a testament to the incredible engineering prowess and unwavering devotion of the ancient Egyptians.

Pyramids served as eternal resting places for the pharaohs, ensuring their transition into the afterlife and eternal glory. Constructing these grand monuments required meticulous planning, an army of skilled laborers, and an unwavering belief in the power of the pharaoh. The sheer scale of these structures and the precision with which they were built continue to baffle modern architects and engineers.

However, the Old Kingdom was not solely defined by pyramid-building. It was a time of great cultural and artistic achievements. Exquisite statues, intricate jewelry, and vibrant wall paintings adorned the palaces and tombs of the pharaohs. The art of the Old Kingdom captured the beauty and grandeur of Egyptian civilization, depicting scenes from everyday life, religious rituals, and the pharaoh's triumphs.

As we explore the Old Kingdom, we will uncover the stories of mighty pharaohs like Djoser, Sneferu, and Khufu, who left an indelible mark on Egyptian history. We will also delve into the lives of the common people, their daily struggles, and the unbreakable bond they shared with their pharaohs.

Join us on this mesmerizing journey through prehistoric civilizations, as we unravel the mysteries of the Old Kingdom. Discover the remarkable legacy of the pharaohs and the enduring wonders they left behind. Let us tread in the footsteps of our ancestors and immerse ourselves in the splendor of ancient Egypt.

The New Kingdom: Ramses the Great and the Empire's Decline

During the New Kingdom period of ancient Egypt, one pharaoh stands out as one of the greatest rulers in the history of civilization -

Ramses the Great. His reign marked the peak of Egyptian power and influence, but it also sowed the seeds of the empire's decline.

Ramses II, also Ramses the Great, ascended to the throne in 1279 BCE and ruled for an astonishing 66 years. He was a prolific builder, leaving behind monumental structures such as the Ramesseum and the Abu Simbel temples. His military campaigns expanded the empire's borders and secured Egypt's dominance in the region.

Under Ramses' rule, Egypt experienced a period of relative stability and prosperity. Trade flourished, and cultural achievements reached new heights. However, the prolonged military campaigns and the grandiose building projects took a toll on the empire's resources.

As Ramses grew older, his reign became marked by a gradual decline in the empire's power. The cost of his ambitious projects drained the treasury, leaving subsequent pharaohs with limited resources to maintain Egypt's vast territories. Additionally, external forces, such as the invasion of the Sea Peoples, put further strain on the empire.

The decline of the New Kingdom can also be attributed to internal factors. The sheer size of the empire made it increasingly difficult to govern effectively. Corruption and bureaucratic inefficiencies plagued the administration, leading to a decline in the quality of governance.

Moreover, Ramses' successors lacked his charisma and leadership skills, resulting in a power vacuum that rivals sought to exploit. The empire faced invasions from various groups, and regional governors began asserting their independence, further fragmenting Egypt's once-unified state.

By the end of the New Kingdom period, Egypt had lost much of its power and influence. The empire had become a shadow of its former glory, and the stage was set for the emergence of new powers in the region.

Despite the decline, Ramses the Great's legacy endured. His grand monuments and military victories left an indelible mark on Egyptian history. Today, his mummified remains still inspire awe and fascination, making him one of the most recognizable figures of ancient Egypt.

The New Kingdom under Ramses the Great witnessed both the apex of Egyptian power and the beginning of its decline. While Ramses' rule brought prosperity and cultural achievements, his ambitious projects and prolonged military campaigns strained the empire's resources. Combined with internal weaknesses and external threats, this ultimately led to the empire's fragmentation and decline. Nevertheless, Ramses the Great's legacy continues to captivate our imaginations, reminding us of the grandeur and eventual fragility of prehistoric civilizations

Egyptian Hieroglyphs

Isis and Horus

Osiris

THE TEMPLE AT KARNAK Egypt

Abu Simbel

Valley of the Kings, Egypt

Chapter Four:

Prehistoric Africa: Kingdoms and Trade Routes

Ancient Nubia and Kush: Trade with Egypt and Axum

In the vast expanse of Africa, where the mighty Nile River flows, lies the ancient land of Nubia and its powerful kingdom of Kush. These prehistoric civilizations have left an indelible mark on the pages of history, with their cultural heritage and significant contributions to trade and commerce.

Nubia, located in present-day Sudan, was an essential crossroads for trade between Egypt and the southern regions of Africa. The Nubians were skilled traders and their strategic location made them a vital link in the commercial network of the ancient world. The Nile River served as their lifeline, providing fertile lands for agriculture and a convenient route for transportation.

Trade between Nubia and Egypt flourished during the New Kingdom period, around 1550 to 1070 BCE. The Nubians supplied Egypt with precious resources such as gold, ivory, ebony, and exotic animal skins, while Egypt, in turn, provided Nubia with grains, linen, and luxury goods. This exchange of goods not only enriched both civilizations but also fostered cultural exchange and diplomatic relations.

One of the most significant trade partners of Nubia and Kush was the ancient kingdom of Axum, located in present-day Ethiopia and Eritrea. Axum was a thriving trading center that connected the Red Sea with the interior of Africa. Through their trade routes, Nubia and Axum exchanged goods, ideas, and cultural practices, leaving a lasting impact on each other's societies.

The trade relationship between Nubia, Axum, and Egypt was not limited to material goods alone. It also facilitated the exchange of knowledge, technology, and religious beliefs. Nubia was greatly influenced by Egyptian civilization, adopting many aspects of their culture, including their writing system, religion, and architectural styles. Similarly, Axum absorbed elements from both Nubia and Egypt, creating a unique blend of cultures that shaped their own civilization.

The trade networks that connected these ancient civilizations played a crucial role in the development of prehistoric societies. They not only stimulated economic growth but also fostered cultural diversity and intellectual exchange. The legacy of Nubia and Kush, intertwined with the trade routes of Egypt and Axum, continues to be a testament to the ingenuity and resilience of our ancestors.

As we journey through the footsteps of these prehistoric civilizations, we come to appreciate the interconnectedness of our world and the profound impact that trade had on shaping the course of history. The story of ancient Nubia and Kush serves as a reminder of the enduring bonds we share with our ancestors and the importance of preserving their rich legacy for future generations to explore and learn from.

Ancient Kush

Ancient Nubia

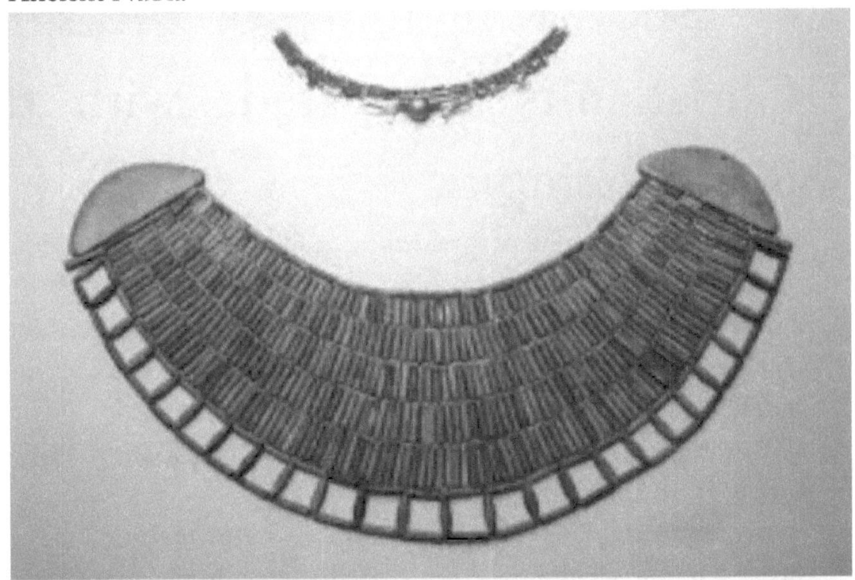

The Kingdom of Aksum: Christianity and Trade with the Roman Empire

In the vast realm of prehistoric civilizations, the Kingdom of Aksum stands tall as a testament to the resilience and ingenuity of our ancestors. Nestled in the northeastern region of Africa, the Aksumite civilization flourished between the 1st and 8th centuries CE, leaving an indelible mark on the history of mankind. One of the defining features of this remarkable kingdom was its unique blend of Christianity and extensive trade with the Roman Empire.

Aksum's conversion to Christianity was a pivotal moment in its history, and it set the stage for a fascinating cultural transformation. During the 4th century CE, King Ezana, inspired by the teachings of Christianity, declared it the official religion of Aksum. This decision not only altered the spiritual landscape of the kingdom but also had profound implications for its trade relations with the Roman Empire.

The adoption of Christianity in Aksum brought about a newfound alliance with the Roman Empire. As the Roman Empire began to embrace Christianity, a strong bond formed between the two powers, fostering a sense of camaraderie and shared values. This religious connection facilitated trade between the two civilizations, with goods flowing from the heart of Africa to the bustling markets of Rome and beyond.

Aksum's strategic location on the Red Sea coast made it a prime hub for maritime trade. Its proximity to the Roman Empire and its access to the Arabian Peninsula made it a vital link in the trade networks of the ancient world. The kingdom's main exports included ivory, gold, spices, and precious stones, while it imported goods such as silk, glassware, and wine from the Roman Empire. This vibrant trade network not only enriched the Aksumite economy but also facilitated the exchange of ideas, technology, and culture.

Through trade, Aksum experienced a profound cultural exchange with the Roman Empire. Christianity, which was a key component of Roman culture, became deeply ingrained in Aksumite society. Churches, monasteries, and religious institutions flourished, making Aksum a bastion of Christianity in Africa. The kingdom's ties with the Roman Empire also influenced its architectural style, art, and language, leaving an enduring legacy on the region's cultural heritage.

The Kingdom of Aksum stands as a testament to the interconnectedness of prehistoric civilizations and the power of cultural exchange. Its adoption of Christianity and flourishing trade with the Roman Empire shaped its destiny and left an indelible mark on its society. As we journey through the footsteps of our ancestors, Aksum serves as a reminder of the rich tapestry of prehistoric civilizations and the enduring legacies they have left behind.

Ancient Aksum

LINDA STANDRIDGE

Chapter Five:

Indus Valley Civilization: Mystery Along the River

The Harappan Culture: Urban Planning and Trade

The Harappan culture, also known as the Indus Valley Civilization, thrived in the northern regions of the Indian subcontinent from approximately 3300 BCE to 1300 BCE. This fascinating prehistoric civilization left behind an impressive legacy, particularly in the areas of urban planning and trade.

One of the most striking features of the Harappan culture was its exceptional urban planning. The cities of Harappa and Mohenjo-Daro stand as evidence of their meticulous approach to city design. These cities were meticulously laid out on a grid system, with well-defined streets and intricate drainage systems that ensured efficient water flow. The Harappans constructed multi-story buildings made of baked bricks, showcasing their architectural brilliance and advanced construction techniques.

The Harappan cities were also home to numerous public buildings, including granaries, bathhouses, and even an impressive citadel. These structures, along with the well-organized residential areas, indicate a society that values community and collective living. The intricate urban planning of the Harappans allowed for efficient use of space and facilitated the development of a well-structured society.

Trade played a vital role in the prosperity of Harappan culture. Excavations have revealed a wide range of artifacts, including pottery, jewelry, and seals, which indicate extensive trade networks. The discovery of seals with symbols and inscriptions suggests a sophisticated system of writing and record-keeping. These seals were likely used to mark goods and facilitate trade across vast distances.

The Harappan people had access to valuable resources such as copper, gold, and semi-precious stones, which were likely traded with other regions. The discovery of Harappan artifacts as far away as

Mesopotamia and Central Asia demonstrates the extent of their trade networks. The exchange of goods and ideas not only fueled economic growth but also contributed to cultural exchange, making the Harappan culture a vibrant and cosmopolitan society.

The Harappan culture stands as a testament to the remarkable achievements of prehistoric civilizations. Their urban planning and trade networks were sophisticated, showcasing their advanced understanding of society and commerce. By exploring the Harappan culture, we gain valuable insights into the complexities of ancient civilizations and the foundations upon which our modern societies are built.

The Decline and Disappearance of the Indus Valley Civilization

The Indus Valley Civilization, one of the most remarkable prehistoric civilizations, flourished along the banks of the Indus River in what is now modern-day Pakistan and northwest India. This ancient society thrived for nearly a thousand years, from around 2500 BCE to 1500 BCE, leaving behind a rich legacy that continues to captivate historians and archaeologists. However, the mysterious decline and ultimate disappearance of this once-great civilization has puzzled experts for decades.

The decline of the Indus Valley Civilization is a complex and multifaceted phenomenon that cannot be attributed to a single cause. Various theories have been put forward by researchers, each offering a unique perspective on the downfall of this magnificent civilization. One prevailing hypothesis suggests that environmental changes, such as a shift in the course of the Indus River or a rise in aridity, may have disrupted the agricultural practices upon which the society depended. This could have led to food scarcity, internal conflicts, and ultimately the collapse of the civilization.

Another theory posits that external invasions played a significant role in the civilization's decline. The presence of fortified cities and evidence of violent destruction in some archeological sites indicate the possibility of invasions by nomadic tribes or rival civilizations. Such invasions could have disrupted trade networks, destroyed infrastructure, and destabilized the social fabric of the Indus Valley society.

Moreover, socio-political factors may have contributed to the decline of this once-thriving civilization. The absence of clear evidence for centralized political authority in the Indus Valley raises questions about the effectiveness of their governance system. Internal power struggles, social unrest, or a loss of faith in the ruling elite could have eroded the stability and cohesion of the society, ultimately leading to its downfall.

Despite numerous theories, the exact reasons behind the disappearance of the Indus Valley Civilization remain elusive. The lack of deciphered written records from this civilization further complicates our understanding of their decline. The enigmatic nature of their script, known as the Indus script, has hindered the interpretation of their language and historical accounts.

Nevertheless, the legacy of the Indus Valley Civilization endures. Its impressive city planning, advanced sanitation systems, and sophisticated craftsmanship are testaments to the ingenuity and creativity of our ancient ancestors. By unraveling the mysteries surrounding their decline, we can gain valuable insights into the complexities of prehistoric civilizations and societies and appreciate the resilience of humanity throughout history.

Harappan remains in Pakistan

Indus Valley Script

Dholavira in India

Dholavira in India

Harappa in Pakistan

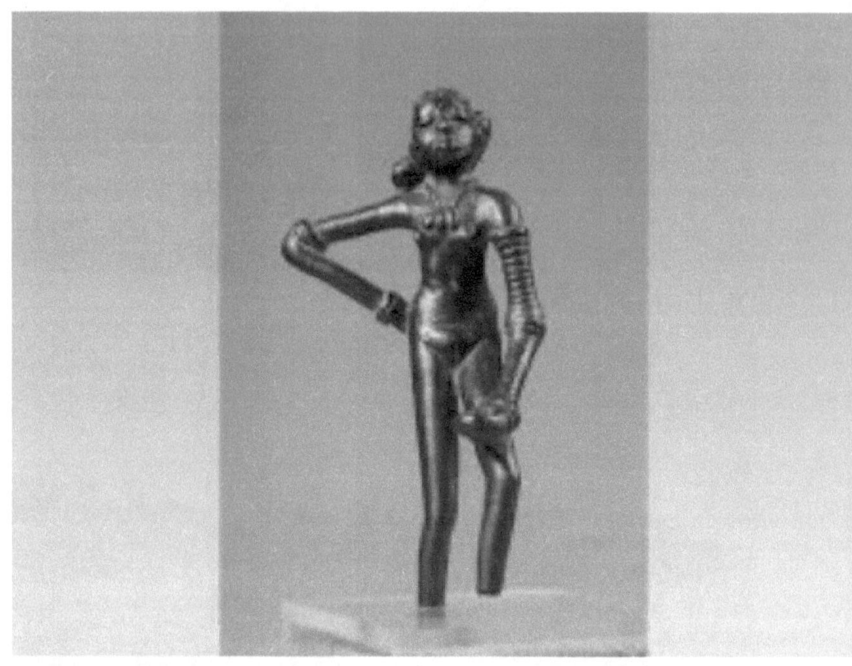

The dancing girl

MOHENJO DARO IN PAKISTAN

Images of Mohenjo-Daro, in Pakistan

Chapter Six:

Ancient China: Dynasties and Philosophies

The Xia and Shang Dynasties: Bronze Age Powers

In the vast tapestry of human history, the Xia and Shang Dynasties stand as early pillars of civilization, their legacies shaping the course of prehistoric civilizations and societies. These Bronze Age powers emerged in ancient China, leaving an indelible mark on the world that would follow.

The Xia Dynasty, believed to have ruled from around 2070 to 1600 BCE, is shrouded in myth and legend. While some historians debate its existence, recent archeological discoveries have shed light on this ancient dynasty. It is said that the Xia Dynasty was founded by Yu the Great, a legendary ruler who tamed the Yellow River and established a centralized government.

During the Xia Dynasty, significant advancements were made in agriculture, craftsmanship, and social organization. Bronze, an alloy of copper and tin, became a hallmark of this era. The Xia people mastered the art of bronze casting, creating exquisite tools and ceremonial objects that showcased their cultural sophistication.

The reign of the Xia Dynasty eventually gave way to the Shang Dynasty, which lasted from around 1600 to 1046 BCE. The Shang Dynasty is remembered as the first confirmed dynasty in Chinese history. It was a period of great cultural and technological progress, with the development of a writing system, elaborate rituals, and a complex social hierarchy.

One of the most remarkable aspects of the Shang Dynasty was its mastery of bronze casting. Bronze vessels, such as wine containers, food vessels, and musical instruments, were not only functional but also served as status symbols. These intricately decorated artifacts demonstrate the advanced metallurgical skills of the Shang people.

The Shang Dynasty also saw the establishment of a centralized bureaucracy and the rise of a powerful ruling class. Oracle bone inscriptions, found on tortoise shells and animal bones, provide valuable insights into the religious and political practices of the time. The divination rituals performed by the Shang rulers, seeking guidance from the ancestors, reveal a belief system deeply rooted in spirituality.

The Xia and Shang Dynasties were pivotal in shaping the early foundations of Chinese civilization. Their mastery of bronze casting, social organization, and cultural practices laid the groundwork for future dynasties and influenced the development of neighboring societies. By studying the Xia and Shang Dynasties, we gain a deeper understanding of our prehistoric ancestors and the remarkable achievements of ancient civilizations.

The Xia

Western Xia Buddhist Temple

Shang dynasty

Anyang, Shang Dynasty city

THE ZHOU DYNASTY: MANDATE of Heaven and Feudalism

In the vast landscape of prehistoric civilizations, the Zhou Dynasty stands as one of the most significant and influential periods in ancient Chinese history. Lasting for over eight centuries, from 1046 to 256 BCE, the Zhou Dynasty witnessed the rise and fall of various dynasties, the development of complex social structures, and the establishment of the Mandate of Heaven and feudalism.

The concept of the Mandate of Heaven played a pivotal role in the Zhou Dynasty's political and religious beliefs. According to this concept, the ruler was chosen by the heavens and enjoyed divine approval as long as they governed in the best interest of the people. The Mandate of Heaven served as a crucial justification for the Zhou Dynasty's authority and legitimacy, allowing it to maintain stability and control over its vast territories.

Feudalism also emerged during the Zhou Dynasty, shaping the social structure and governance of ancient China. Under the feudal system, the ruler granted land and power to nobles and aristocrats in exchange for their loyalty and military support. This decentralized system helped the Zhou Dynasty govern its vast territories more efficiently and effectively.

The Zhou Dynasty's feudal system consisted of three main social classes: the king and his family, the nobles and aristocrats, and the commoners. The king, known as the Son of Heaven, held the highest authority and was responsible for maintaining harmony and order in society. The nobles and aristocrats were given fiefs and were expected to provide military service and support to the king. The commoners, comprising the majority of the population, were responsible for agriculture, craftsmanship, and other essential tasks to sustain the kingdom.

The Middle Kingdom: Expansion and Cultural Flourishing

During ancient times, a remarkable civilization existed that thrived in what is now known as China. The Middle Kingdom was a period characterized by vast expansion and cultural flourishing. Join us on a journey through the prehistoric civilizations of China, as we delve into the fascinating history of this remarkable era.

The Middle Kingdom witnessed an unprecedented expansion of its territory. The ruling dynasties, such as the Shang and the Zhou, embarked on ambitious conquests, gradually annexing neighboring regions and establishing an empire that stretched beyond what was previously thought possible. This expansion not only brought new lands under Chinese control but also allowed for the exchange of ideas and cultural practices with diverse populations.

With the acquisition of new territories came an influx of various ethnic groups, leading to a melting pot of cultures and traditions. The Middle Kingdom became a vibrant hub of cultural exchange, fostering the growth of art, literature, and philosophy. The era saw the development of intricate bronze casting techniques, which produced exquisite ritual objects and weapons. These artifacts not only served practical purposes but also held symbolic significance, reflecting the spiritual beliefs of the time.

Literature and philosophy flourished during this period, with the emergence of renowned thinkers such as Confucius and Laozi. Their teachings, emphasizing social order, moral conduct, and harmonious living, laid the foundation for Chinese society for centuries to come. The writings of these great minds continue to inspire and shape the moral fabric of Chinese culture even today.

The Middle Kingdom also witnessed advancements in agriculture and technology. The introduction of iron tools revolutionized farming practices, leading to increased productivity and the ability to sustain a growing population. The construction of an irrigation system and the development of sophisticated pottery techniques further contributed to the prosperity of the civilization.

As we journey through the prehistoric civilizations of China, the Middle Kingdom stands out as a remarkable era of expansion and cultural flourishing. Its legacy can be seen in the enduring traditions, philosophical principles, and artistic achievements that continue to shape Chinese civilization.

The Zhou Dynasty's emphasis on feudalism and the Mandate of Heaven fostered a unique socio-political structure. However, over time, this system began to crumble, leading to internal conflicts and external threats. The decline of the Zhou Dynasty eventually paved the way for the rise of subsequent Chinese dynasties, such as the Qin and Han Dynasties.

Understanding the Zhou Dynasty's Mandate of Heaven and feudalism provides us with valuable insights into the evolution of prehistoric civilizations and societies. It showcases the intricate balance between religious beliefs, political power, and social hierarchies that shaped ancient China.

THE ZHOU DYNASTY

The Forbidden City

The Qin and Han Dynasties: The Great Wall and the Silk Road

The Qin and Han Dynasties were two significant periods in ancient Chinese history. These dynasties witnessed the construction of the Great Wall and the development of the Silk Road, two remarkable achievements that shaped the region's culture, economy, and international relations.

During the Qin Dynasty (221-206 BCE), the first emperor of unified China, Qin Shi Huangdi, ordered the construction of the Great Wall. This monumental project aimed to protect the empire's northern borders from invasions by nomadic tribes. The Great Wall, stretching over 13,000 miles, was an engineering marvel, utilizing various materials such as stone, rammed earth, and wood. It served both as a physical barrier and a symbol of imperial power. Although it did not completely prevent invasions, it served as a deterrent and a testament to the Qin Dynasty's dominance.

His last great monument was a gigantic funerary compound, of some 20 square miles, hewn out of a mountain and shaped in conformity with the symbolic patterns of the cosmos. Among the grave goods found were two bronze chariots along with a life-size terracotta army of 10,000 soldiers and hundreds of horses. No one knows what the mausoleum might hold for it hasn't been opened. Sima Qian wrote in the late 2nd century to early 1st century about the tomb of the first emperor. "Mercury was used to fashion the hundred rivers, the Yellow River and the Yangtze River, and the seas in such a way they flowed." The idea is that the main burial chamber is a replica of China (as it was then) with rivers, lakes, and seas of shimmering mercury.

The Han Dynasty (206 BCE- 220 CE), further expanded the Great Wall and strengthened its fortifications. This period also witnessed the establishment and flourishing of the Silk Road. The Silk Road was a network of trade routes connecting China with the Western world, facilitating the exchange of goods, ideas, and cultures. Its name derives from the lucrative trade in Chinese silk, which played a central role in the economic prosperity of the Han Dynasty.

The Silk Road extended for thousands of miles, passing through diverse landscapes and connecting various civilizations, such as China, India, Persia, and Rome. Along the route, merchants traded not only silk but also other commodities such as spices, precious metals, and exotic animals. This exchange of goods also led to the transmission of knowledge, technology, and religious beliefs, fostering cultural exchange between East and West.

The Silk Road's impact extended beyond commerce. It stimulated innovation in transportation, leading to the introduction of the camel as the primary means of transportation through the harsh desert terrains. Furthermore, it facilitated the spread of Buddhism from India to China, profoundly influencing Chinese philosophy, art, and architecture.

The Qin and Han dynasties left a lasting legacy through their monumental achievements. The Great Wall and the Silk Road not only played crucial roles in shaping China's history but also had a profound impact on the development of prehistoric civilizations and societies. They stand as a testament to the ingenuity, ambition, and interconnectedness of our ancient ancestors.

THE QIN DYNASTY

The tomb of the first Emperor Qin Shi Huang

LINDA STANDRIDGE

The Great Wall
The Han Dynasty

LINDA STANDRIDGE

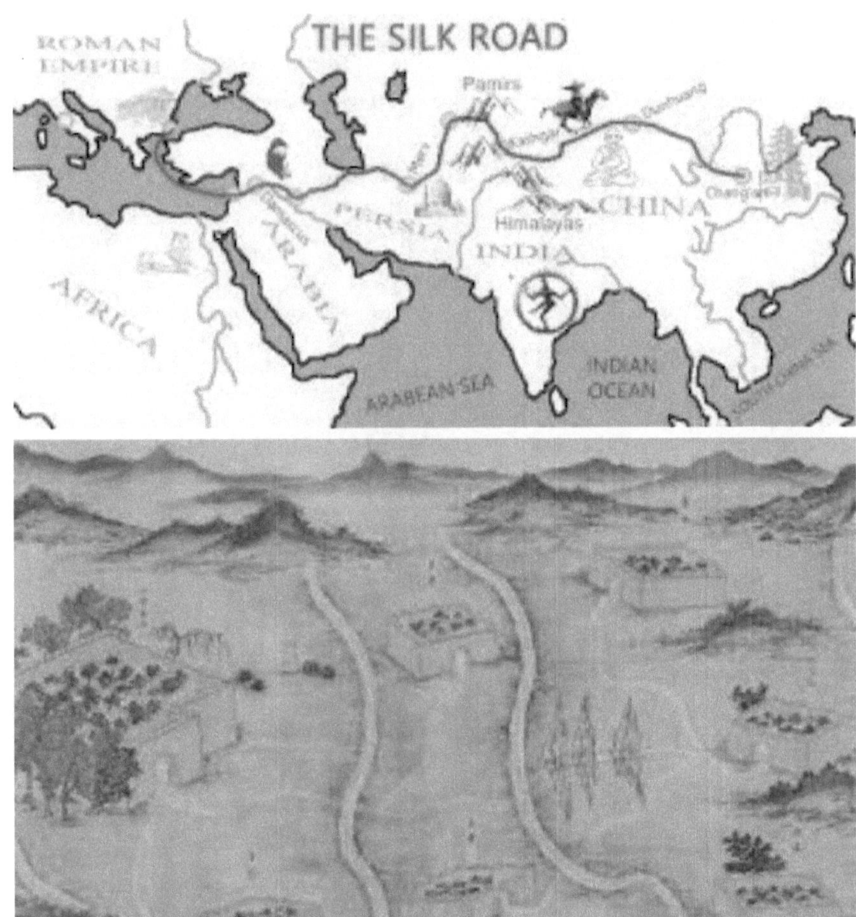
THE SILK ROAD
ROMAN EMPIRE
Pamirs
Dunhuang
PERSIA
ARABIA
Himalayas
CHINA
INDIA
Chang'an
AFRICA
ARABEAN SEA
INDIAN OCEAN

Mesoamerica: Ancient Cultures of the Americas

The Olmecs: Mother Culture of Mesoamerica

The Olmecs, often referred to as the "mother culture" of Mesoamerica, were a prehistoric civilization that thrived in what is now modern-day Mexico from around 1500 to 400 BCE. Their influence on subsequent societies in the region cannot be overstated, as they laid the foundation for many aspects of Mesoamerican culture, including art, architecture, religion, and trade.

The Olmecs were known for their advanced agricultural techniques, which allowed them to sustain a large population and establish sedentary communities. They developed irrigation systems, cultivated maize, beans, and squash, and traded these surplus crops with neighboring communities. This agricultural surplus enabled the growth of complex social hierarchies and the emergence of a ruling elite.

One of the most iconic features of the Olmec culture is their colossal stone heads, which are believed to depict the Olmec rulers. These massive stone sculptures, weighing up to 40 tons, showcase the Olmec's exceptional craftsmanship and artistic skill. The heads also indicate the centralized political power of the Olmec rulers and their reverence for their leaders.

In addition to their monumental art, the Olmecs were pioneers in the development of a writing system. Though not yet fully deciphered, their hieroglyphic script is evidence of their intellectual prowess and the complexity of their society. They also invented a calendar system that served as the basis for subsequent Mesoamerican calendars.

Religion played a significant role in Olmec society, as evidenced by their extensive temple complexes and religious iconography. The Olmecs worship a pantheon of deities, including a jaguar god and a rain god, reflecting their dependence on agriculture. Ritual bloodletting and human sacrifice were also integral parts of their religious practices.

The Olmecs' influence extended beyond their immediate region, as their trade networks connected them with other Mesoamerican societies. They traded goods such as jade, obsidian, and rubber, which were highly prized commodities at the time. This exchange of goods facilitated cultural exchange and helped spread Olmec's ideas and traditions throughout the Mesoamerican region.

Although the Olmec civilization eventually declined, their legacy lived on in subsequent Mesoamerican cultures such as the Maya and the Aztecs. The Olmecs laid the groundwork for the sophisticated civilizations that would follow, leaving an indelible mark on the history of Mesoamerica.

The Olmecs were a remarkable prehistoric civilization that laid the foundation for Mesoamerican culture. Their advanced agricultural techniques, monumental art, writing system, religious practices, and extensive trade networks cemented their status as the "mother culture" of Mesoamerica. By studying the Olmecs, we gain valuable insights into the origins of complex societies and the interconnectedness of prehistoric civilizations.

The Olmec Civilization

The Maya: Astronomy and Hieroglyphics

The Maya civilization, one of the most enigmatic and advanced prehistoric societies, left an indelible mark on history with their remarkable achievements in astronomy and hieroglyphics. The intricate knowledge and remarkable skills demonstrated by the Maya in these fields continue to astound researchers and archeologists to this day.

Astronomy played a central role in the daily lives of the Maya people. They developed an incredibly accurate calendar system that allowed them to track celestial events with unparalleled precision. With their advanced understanding of astronomical phenomena, they were able to predict eclipses, solstices, and equinoxes, which were of utmost importance for agricultural planning and religious ceremonies. This intimate connection between the Maya and the cosmos illustrates their deep respect for nature and their ability to harmonize with the celestial forces.

Furthermore, the Maya constructed elaborate observatories and architectural structures aligned with celestial bodies. The most famous example is the Temple of Kukulkan at Chichen Itza, Where the sun's light casts a shadow on the pyramid in the shape of a serpent during the equinoxes. This incredible architectural feat serves as a testament to the Maya's profound knowledge of astronomy and their ability to integrate it into their built environment.

Hieroglyphics, another remarkable aspect of Maya culture, allowed them to record and communicate their history, religious beliefs, and scientific knowledge. The Maya developed a complex writing system that consisted of thousands of unique characters, each representing a word, a syllable, or even a concept. This sophisticated system enabled them to document their astronomical observations, record historical events, and pass down their knowledge from generation to generation.

Deciphering the Maya hieroglyphics has been a significant challenge for scholars, but recent breakthroughs have shed light on their incredible achievements. The discovery of the Rosetta Stone of the Maya, the Hieroglyphic Stairway at Copan, greatly aided researchers in deciphering the intricate writing system. Today we can appreciate the depth of their knowledge and the intricacies of their culture through the translated hieroglyphic texts.

The Maya's mastery of astronomy and hieroglyphics is a testament to their advanced understanding of the natural world and their ability to create complex systems of communication. BY delving into the mysteries of the Maya civilization, we can gain a deeper appreciation for the rich tapestry of prehistoric civilizations and societies that have shaped our world. The Maya's remarkable achievements continue to inspire awe and wonder, reminding us of the incredible potential of human ingenuity and the profound beauty of our shared human history.

The Mayan Civilization

Mayan hieroglyphs

The Dresden codex Maya hieroglyphs

Death Mask of Pakal the Great

EL CARACOL, CHICHEN Itza, Mexico

Teotihuacan north of Mexico City

Temple of the Sun

Pyramid of Kukulkan

Temple of the Inscriptions in Palenque

Chapter Eight:

The Pre-Inca: The Chavin, The Nazca, and the Moche

The Chavin

The Chavin civilization was the first major unifying culture in what is modern-day Peru. The Chavin civilization rose to prominence in approximately 1000 BCE. The site known as Chavin de Huantar is thought to be the center of the Chavin civilization and is the site that gave this culture its name. At this time we don't know what the Chavin called themselves. It has been speculated that the Chavin may have originated in the lowlands by the Amazon River. Some of the creatures depicted in Chavin's religious art came from the lowlands not in the Andes.

The Chavin civilization was home to many skilled artisans who were skilled in pottery, textiles, stone, and precious metals. The Chavins were also skilled architects. They built canals, monumental temples, and subterranean galleries that appear to have been designed for acoustics. There is no evidence yet found for their rulers or military.

The Chavin built temples with a complex underground system of tunnels and rooms. Little is known about their religious practices, no details have survived. The only item is a stela known as the Lanzon. Upon the stela is a depiction of an anthropomorphic jaguar deity, leading archeologists to speculate the existence of a jaguar cult.

The Chavin civilization began to decline approximately 200 BCE. There is no clear reason for the decline or the abandonment of their settlements. What is clear is that their artistic influence dominated the area and was a major influence on the civilizations that followed.

The Chavin civilization

Chavin de Huantar

The Nazca

The Nazca (Nasca) civilization appeared in approximately 200 BCE on the southern coast of Peru. It is believed that they were an offshoot of the earlier Paracas culture. They thrived for approximately 500 years in an arid desert region prone to drought, earthquakes, and floods.

The Nazca were unique among ancient civilizations. They etched massive geoglyphs into the landscape. The exact purpose of the geoglyphs is unknown. One hypothesis is they were ceremonial walkways related to the distribution and consumption of water. Water was central to their religion, it is only natural in such a hostile environment.

Ancient Alien enthusiasts tend to speculate that the lines were landing strips for an ancient craft. In fact, archaeological evidence has shown that the Nazca created the line by a simple system of measurement using ropes of various lengths and the Nazca moving rocks and scraping away the surface layer of desert sand to create the design. Who the designs were meant for is unclear. Archeologists speculate that it was meant to be seen from nearby mountains and hills. Ancient Alien enthusiasts say that it can only be seen clearly from the air. Since humans did not have the ability to fly before the 20th Century, It had to be for our alien ancestors. I lean more toward the scientific explanation, but I could be wrong.

It is believed that Cahuachi was the center of religious power. The Nazca had a complex water management system consisting of cisterns and underground aqueducts. There isn't any evidence of residential districts in Cahuachi. However, there are a large number of burial mounds and graves with rich offerings found at the site.

The Nazca practiced human sacrifice and ancestor worship. Archeologists have excavated "trophy heads" at ceremonial sites. Also, Nazca pottery and textiles were found with motifs of trophy heads.

Considering the hostile environment the Nazca lived in, it has been speculated that these were sacrifices to appease the spirits, deities, or natural forces that surrounded them.

Ultimately, it was the environment that spelled doom for the Nazca civilization. In approximately 500 CE, a massive El Nino hit the area causing massive floods that destroyed much of their infrastructure and farmland. For a culture that held water in such reverence, it was an ironic end.

The Nazca Civilization

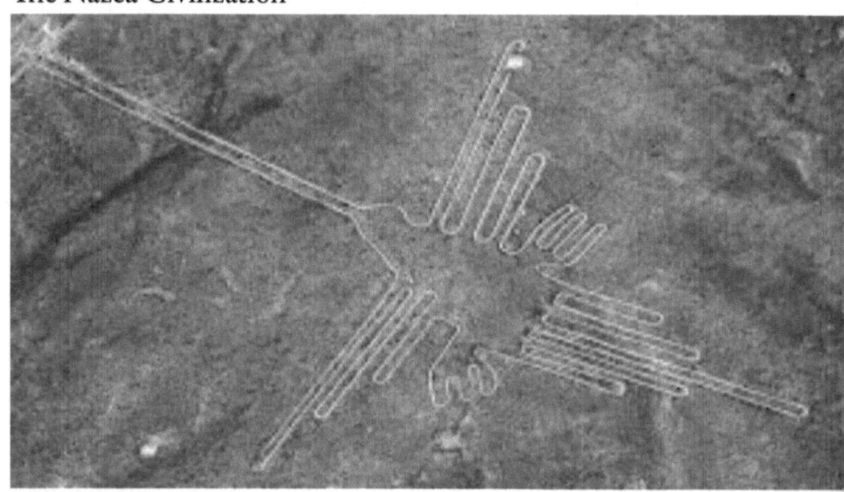

The Hummingbird

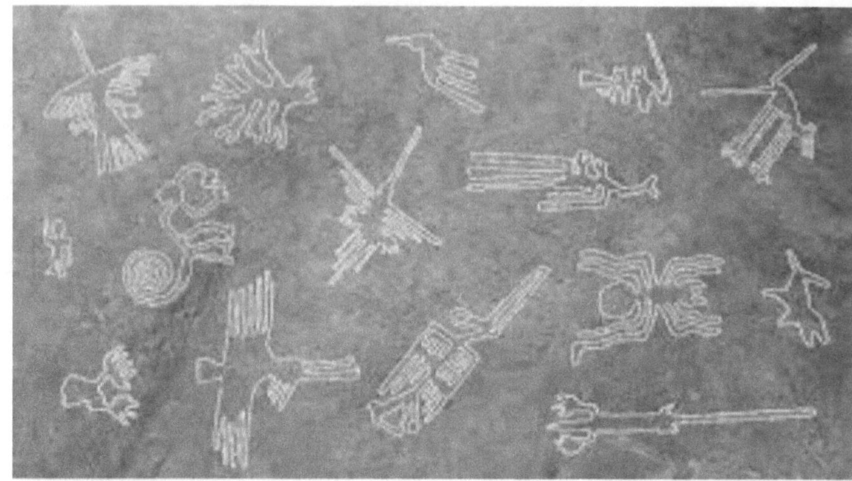

Cahuachi

The Moche

The heart of the Moche civilization was a vast temple-city complex called the Huaca De La Luna–the temple of the moon. The temple was dedicated to the Moche god of the mountains, Aiapaec. Huaca De La Luna was lavishly decorated with colorful frescoes.

The Moche culture was a group of loosely unified chiefdoms. It is speculated that each chiefdom was led by a Warrior Priest, who brought prisoners of war to the temple. These prisoners would then be sacrificed, and their blood collected in cups from which the Warrior Priests would drink.

The Moche were also skilled architects and artisans. They built their temples, palaces, administrative buildings, and homes out of adobe bricks. Some of the buildings were decorated with colorful frescoes. The buildings were almost completely destroyed by the Conquistadors. Thankfully, much of the Moches' incredible pottery survived. It is considered to be the most lifelike art found anywhere else in ancient America. They were also skilled metallurgists who pioneered a range of gilding and soldering techniques. They made elaborate headdresses, body jewelry, and ceremonial objects.

The Moche were a contemporary civilization with the Nazca. It is believed that the El Nino that destroyed the Nazca civilization signaled the end of the Moche. The fall of the Moche took place over an extended period. As resources became scarce, the different chiefdoms likely turned on each other, until all former cultural ties were severed by war.

The Moche Civilization

The Lord of Sipan

The Tiwanaku

As the Nazcas and the Moche civilizations went into decline, far to the south, on the shores of Lake Titicaca, approximately 550 CE the Tiwanaku Civilization grew to prominence. The capital city of Tiwanaku was home to 30,000 residents.

The Tiwanaku were sophisticated agricultural engineers, who transformed over 45,000 acres into a raised-bed irrigation system that fed their population and produced a surplus.

Their architects and stonemasons produced monumental stonework held together with bronze clamps. Beautiful, carved reliefs decorated their sacred spaces.

The Tiwanaku architecture, sculpture, roads, and empire management influenced many civilizations that would follow. The Tiwanaku civilization was incorporated into the Incan mythology. They believed that their great Creator god Viracocha emerged from Lake Titicaca.

THE TIWANAKU CIVILIZATION

PUMA PUNKU IN BOLIVIA

Unsolved mystery at Puma Punku

Chapter Nine:

Prehistoric Europe: From Megaliths to Iron Age

Stonehenge and Other Megalithic Monuments

Prehistoric civilizations and societies have always fascinated us with their awe-inspiring monuments, and none is more captivating than Stonehenge. This enigmatic stone circle situated on Salisbury Plain, England, has mystified archaeologists, historians, and enthusiasts alike for centuries.

Stonehenge stands as an enduring testament to the ingenuity and vision of our prehistoric ancestors. Its construction commenced around 3000 BCE, and it went through several phases of development over the following millennia. Composed of massive standing stones, some weighing up to 25 tons, Stonehenge's purpose remains shrouded in mystery. Was it an ancient astronomical observatory, a sacred burial ground, or a place of ritual and ceremony? We examine the latest research and theories surrounding this iconic monument, shedding light on its significance and purpose.

But Stonehenge is not alone in the realm of megalithic wonders. Throughout the world, ancient civilizations left their mark in the form of awe-inspiring stone structures. From the massive stone heads of Easter Island to the towering obelisks of ancient Egypt, these monuments offer a glimpse into the beliefs, rituals, and social structures of our ancestors.

We journey to the remote Orkney Islands in Scotland, where the impressive standing stones of the Ring of Brodgar and the chambered tomb of Maeshowe stand as testaments to an ancient Neolithic society. We explore the intricate stone carvings of the Tumulus of Bougon in France, which date back over 6,000 years. And we uncover the secrets of the ancient stone circles of Avebury and Callanish, which rival Stonehenge in their grandeur and significance.

Through stunning photographs, expert analysis, and captivating storytelling, we invite you to step into the footsteps of our ancestors and unravel the mysteries of these prehistoric civilizations. Discover the remarkable ingenuity and profound spirituality that drove our ancient forebears to create these enduring megalithic monuments.

The Celtic civilization

Stonehenge on the Salisbury Plain, England

Skara Brae in Orkney, Scotland

Skara Brae in Orkney, Scotland

Carnac Stones in Brittany, France

The Celts: Druids and Warrior Culture

The Celtic civilization is one of the most captivating and enigmatic prehistoric societies that ever existed. Nestled in the heart of Europe, the Celts thrived during the Iron Age, leaving behind a legacy that still captures the imagination of people today. At the core of their society were the Druids, the revered spiritual leaders who played a pivotal role in shaping Celtic beliefs and customs.

The Druids held a sacred position within Celtic society. They were the keepers of knowledge, serving as priests, judges, healers, and advisors to the ruling elite. Their wisdom and influence extended beyond religious matters, as they were also responsible for educating the young and preserving the oral traditions of the Celts. The Druids were deeply connected to nature and believed in the power of the elements. They conducted rituals in sacred groves and performed ceremonies at sacred sites, such as Stonehenge and Avebury.

Warfare was an integral part of Celtic society, and their warrior culture was renowned throughout the ancient world. Celtic warriors were fierce, skilled, and often fought naked, adorned with intricate body art to intimidate their enemies. They valued bravery and individual prowess, and their combat techniques were highly developed. The Celts excelled in chariot warfare, using their superior horsemanship and agility to their advantage.

Celtic society was organized into small, tightly-knit communities led by chieftains. These communities were fiercely independent, yet connected through a shared Celtic identity and language. The Celts had a vibrant trading network, spreading their influence across Europe and interacting with other cultures. They were skilled artisans, known for their intricate metalwork, jewelry, and weaponry. The famous

Celtic knotwork, with its intricate patterns and symbolism, still captivates artists and designers to this day.

However, the Celts faced challenges from the expanding Roman Empire, which sought to subjugate their lands. The Romans, impressed by their culture and warrior spirit, eventually conquered the Celts, leading to the assimilation of Celtic traditions into Roman society.

Studying the Celts and their Druids offers a glimpse into a unique time and place in history. Their spirituality, warrior culture, and artistic achievements continue to inspire and intrigue adults interested in the mysteries of prehistoric civilizations. Exploring the legacy of the Celts allows us to connect with our ancient ancestors and appreciate the rich tapestry of human history that preceded us.

The Greeks and Romans: Influence on European Civilization

In the vast tapestry of European civilization, few threads have been as significant and enduring as the influence of the ancient Greeks and Romans.

Their contributions spanned the realms of art, philosophy, politics, and literature, leaving an indelible mark on the course of history.

The ancient Greeks cultivated a society that placed great emphasis on intellectual pursuits. Their philosophers, such as Socrates, Plato, and Aristotle, laid the groundwork for Western philosophy, questioning the nature of reality, ethics, and the best forms of governance. Their ideas continue to shape our thinking today, influencing fields as diverse as science, politics, and ethics.

The Greek's artistic achievements were equally remarkable. Their sculptures, characterized by an idealized depiction of the human form, still captivate us with their beauty and realism. The architectural wonder of the Parthenon in Athens stands as a testament to their architectural prowess, while their dramatic plays and poetry continue to inspire modern literature.

The Romans, on the other hand, excelled in engineering, governance, and law. Their mastery of infrastructure is evident in the construction of roads, aqueducts, and monumental structures like the Colosseum. The Roman legal system, based on the principles of fairness and equality, laid the foundation for modern legal systems worldwide.

Another significant contribution of both civilizations was their rich mythological traditions. These captivating tales of gods and heroes, not only entertained, but also provided a moral framework for their societies. Many of these myths have endured through the ages, woven into the fabric of European literature and art.

Furthermore, the Romans' expansionist tendencies led to the spread of their language, Latin, throughout Europe. Latin became the lingua franca of scholars, facilitating the exchange of knowledge and ideas across borders. Even today, Latin influences many European languages, particularly in terms of vocabulary and grammar.

The impact of the Greeks and Romans on European civilization cannot be overstated. Their legacy permeates every aspect of our lives, from our political systems to our artistic sensibilities. By understanding their contributions, we gain insight into the origins of our own society and can better appreciate the richness and diversity of our European heritage.

The Roman civilization

The Colosseum

A Roman Aqueduct

Roman script

ROMAN MOSAICS

Pompeii
The Greek empire

The Acropolis

Chapter Ten:

Oceania: Island Hopping Across the Pacific

The Lapita Culture: Ancestral Polynesia

The Lapita culture, an ancient civilization that flourished in the Pacific region, holds a significant place in the study of prehistoric civilizations and societies. The Lapita culture emerged around 1500 BCE, spanning from the Bismarck Archipelago in the west to Fiji in the east. They were skilled seafarers, navigating vast ocean expenses in sturdy outrigger canoes, and eventually settling in various island groups across the Pacific. Their remarkable voyages laid the foundation for the Polynesian expansion, shaping the cultural landscape of the region.

One of the striking aspects of the Lapita culture was their distinctive pottery. Characterized by intricate geometric designs, these ceramics showcased the artistic flair and technical expertise of their creators. The distribution of Lapita pottery across different islands provides valuable insights into their migration patterns and cultural exchange networks.

Beyond their pottery, the Lapita people left behind an array of archeological evidence, including tools, shell ornaments, and human remains. These artifacts shed light on their lifestyle, subsistence strategies, and social organization. For instance, the presence of fishhooks and shellfish remains suggests a reliance on marine resources, while the discovery of ceremonial objects implies the existence of religious or ritual practices.

Moreover, recent genetic studies have provided fascinating insights into the ancestry of Polynesians. By analyzing the DNA of present-day populations and comparing it to ancient Lapita remains, scientists have traced the genetic links between the Lapita culture and modern-day Polynesians. These findings have not only deepened our understanding of human migration but also reinforced the cultural continuity that connects the past with the present.

The Lapita culture represents a crucial chapter in the story of prehistoric civilizations and societies. Their seafaring abilities, artistic achievements, and cultural contributions laid the groundwork for the vibrant Polynesian cultures that emerged later. Exploring the Lapita legacy not only enriches our knowledge of our ancestors but also highlights the remarkable accomplishments of a civilization that shaped the Pacific region as we know it today.

Lapita Civilization

Rapa Nui script (Easter Island)

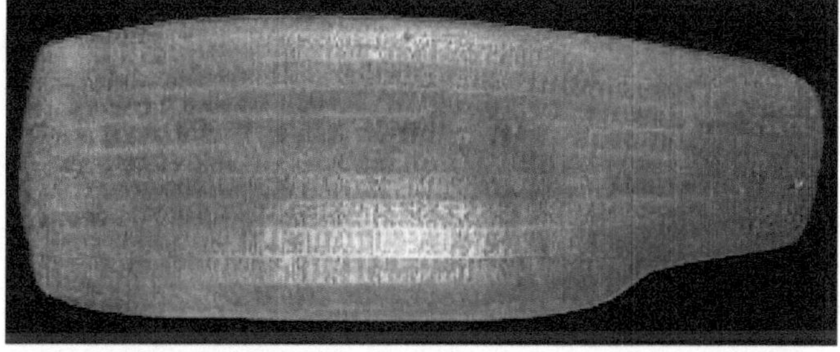

Rongorongo

The Maori: Indigenous People of New Zealand

The Maori people of the indigenous inhabitants of New Zealand, and their rich culture and history are deeply intertwined with the land they call home. The Maori have a remarkable oral tradition that stretches back centuries, passed down through generations to preserve their history and customs. According to their legends, their ancestors arrived in New Zealand for Hawaiki, a mythical Polynesian homeland, around a thousand years ago. They braved treacherous oceans in canoes, navigating by the stars and the knowledge of their seafaring skills. This incredible journey is considered one of the most significant migrations in human history.

Upon arrival, the Maori settled in various regions, establishing tribal communities and forming complex social structures. Their society was organized into iwi (tribes), each with its own distinct customs, language, and territory. These tribes were led by chiefs, who held significant power and were responsible for making decisions that affected their people's welfare.

One of the most recognizable aspects of Maori culture is their art and craftsmanship. From intricate wood carvings to elaborate tattoos known as moko, the Maori have developed a unique artistic style that reflects their deep spiritual beliefs and connection to nature. Their art often incorporates symbols and motifs that tell stories and represent their ancestral heritage.

Additionally, the Maori have a rich tradition of storytelling through song and dance. Their performances, known as Kapa haka, are a mesmerizing display of vocal harmonies, rhythmic movements, and facial expressions. These cultural expressions serve as a way of preserving their history, passing on knowledge, and connecting with their ancestors.

Unfortunately, the arrival of European settlers in the 18th century brought significant challenges for the Maori people. Land disputes, disease, and cultural assimilation threatened their way of life. However, in recent decades there has been a resurgence of Maori pride and cultural revival, with efforts to preserve their language, customs, and land rights.

Today, the Maori continue to play a vital role in shaping New Zealand's identity and society. Their contributions to prehistoric civilizations include their navigational skills, artistry, and rich cultural heritage. By understanding and appreciating the Maori's unique perspective on the world, we gain valuable insights into the interconnectedness of humanity and the importance of preserving our diverse cultural heritage. We must recognize the Maori as one of the world's prehistoric civilizations, embracing their wisdom and fascinating contributions to our shared human history.

Maori civilization

Traditional Maori tattoo

200-year-old Maori drawing

MAORI CAVE ART

The Aboriginal Australians: Ancient Art and Dreamtime

The Aboriginal Australians hold a significant place in the annals of prehistoric civilizations. With a rich cultural heritage and deep connection to their land, they have left behind a legacy of ancient art and a complex belief system known as Dreamtime. We will delve into the fascinating world of the Aboriginal Australians, exploring their artistic expressions and the spiritual realm they inhabited.

The ancient art of the Aboriginal Australians is a testament to their profound connection to the natural world. Their artwork, often found on rock shelters and cave walls, is characterized by intricate patterns, vibrant colors, and deep symbolism. It tells stories of creation, ancestral spirits, and the sacred relationship between humans and the land. These art forms, spanning thousands of years, provide a window into the lives and beliefs of this ancient civilization.

One of the key concepts in Aboriginal culture is Dreamtime, also known as the Dreaming or Alcheringa. Dreamtime refers to both the ancestral period of creation and the ongoing spiritual dimension that underpins Aboriginal life. According to their belief system, the world was created by ancestral beings who shaped the land, animals, and plants. These ancestral beings continue to exist in the Dreaming, guiding, and influencing the lives of present-day Aboriginal people.

Dreamtime is not just a religious or mythological concept; it is an integral part of everyday life for Aboriginal Australians. It influences their rituals, customs, and social structures. Through ceremonies, storytelling, and songlines, which are ancient routes that connect significant sites across the landscape, Aboriginal people maintain their spiritual connection to the Dreaming and possess their ancestral knowledge to future generations.

Exploring ancient art and understanding the concept of Dreamtime allows us to appreciate the depth and complexity of the Aboriginal Australian culture. It provides insights into their intimate relationship with the natural world, their reverence for ancestral beings, and their profound spiritual beliefs. By immersing ourselves in their rich cultural heritage, we gain a greater understanding of our human origins and the diversity of prehistoric civilizations.

In conclusion, the Aboriginal Australians' ancient art and the concept of Dreamtime are captivating aspects of their civilization. By examining their artistic expressions and delving into their spiritual beliefs, we gain a deep appreciation for the Aboriginal culture and its unique place in the tapestry of prehistoric civilizations

AUSTRALIAN ABORIGINAL civilization

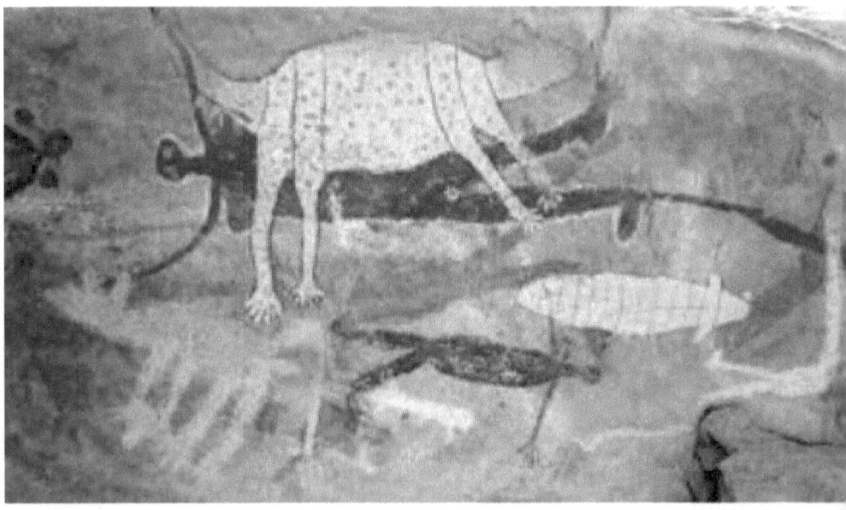

Chapter Eleven:

Unraveling the Mysteries: Archaeology and Discoveries

Archaeological Techniques and Methods

In the fascinating world of prehistoric civilizations and societies, exploring the remnants of our ancestors requires a range of specialized techniques and methods. Archaeologists play a crucial role in unraveling the mysteries of the past, piecing together the stories of ancient cultures, and shedding light on the lives of those who came before us. We will discuss the various archaeological techniques and methods employed by these intrepid researchers.

Excavation is perhaps the most well-known and essential technique in archaeology. Through careful and systematic digging, archaeologists unearth artifacts, structures, and even entire settlements buried beneath the ground. This meticulous process requires patience and attention to detail, as every layer of soil holds valuable information about the past.

Once artifacts are discovered, they are carefully documented and analyzed. An array of methods is employed to determine the age, origin, and purpose of these objects. Carbon dating, for example, allows archaeologists to estimate the age of organic remains by analyzing the decay of carbon isotopes. Similarly, dendrochronology utilizes tree-ring patterns to establish the age of wooden artifacts.

Beyond the excavation site, remote sensing techniques are employed to detect buried remains without disturbing the ground. Ground-penetrating radar, for instance, uses electromagnetic waves to create subsurface images, revealing hidden structures and features that may be missed during excavation. Aerial photography and satellite imagery also provide invaluable insights into the landscape and help identify potential archaeological sites.

Archaeologists also rely on experimental archaeology, which involves reconstructing ancient tools, buildings, and even ancient techniques to gain a deeper understanding of the past. By replicating these artifacts and processes, researchers can test hypotheses, explore practicalities, and gain insights into the daily lives of our ancestors.

Another crucial aspect of archaeological research is the study of human remains. Bioarchaeologists use a combination of techniques such as osteology and DNA analysis to study ancient bones and teeth. By examining the remains, researchers can uncover valuable information aboutthe health, diet, and even migration patterns of past societies.

Overall, the techniques and methods employed in archaeology are as diverse as the civilizations they seek to unravel. Through excavation, remote sensing, experimental archaeology, and the study of human remains, archaeologists piece together the puzzle of our prehistoric ancestors. By understanding these techniques, we not only gain a window into the past but also appreciate the immense dedication and expertise required to unlock the secrets of our ancient civilizations.

FAMOUS ARCHAEOLOGICAL Sites and Discoveries

In the vast expanse of time, our ancestors have left behind remarkable traces of their existence. Through the tireless efforts of archaeologists, we have been able to unearth and decipher the stories of prehistoric civilizations. We will delve into the most famous archaeological sites and discoveries that offer a glimpse into the fascinating world of our ancient forebears.

One such iconic site is the ancient city of Pompeii, frozen in time by the catastrophic eruption of Mount Vesuvius in 79 AD. This Roman city, buried under layers of ash and pumice, was remarkably preserved, allowing us to explore the daily lives and customs of its inhabitants. From the intricately decorated villas to the preserved frescoes and mosaics, Pompeii provides a unique window into the lives of the Romans.

Moving further back in time, the Stonehenge monument in England stands as an enigmatic testament to the ingenuity of our ancestors. Constructed over 4,500 years ago, this ancient stone circle continues to captivate researchers and visitors alike. The purpose of this monumental structure remains a subject of debate, with theories ranging from religious rituals to astronomical observatories. Regardless of its original intent, Stonehenge is an awe-inspiring testament to the engineering skills and cultural significance of its builders.

Heading to the Americas, the ancient Maya civilization has left a rich legacy of archaeological sites. One of the most famous is Chichen Itza in Mexico. This expansive complex features the iconic El Castillo pyramid, which serves as a remarkable astronomical calendar. During the equinoxes, the play of light and shadow creates the illusion of a serpent slithering down the steps——a testament to the Maya's advanced understanding of celestial events.

The discovery of the tomb of Tutankhamun in the Valley of the Kings in Egypt is another archaeological milestone. Discovered by Howard Carter in 1922, this well-preserved burial chamber contained a treasure trove of ancient artifacts, providing unprecedented insights into the opulence and religious beliefs of the ancient Egyptians.

These are just a few of the countless archaeological sites and discoveries that have shaped our understanding of prehistoric civilizations. Each excavation offers a unique piece of the puzzle, allowing us to unravel the mysteries of our ancestors' lives. As we continue to explore and unearth these ancient wonders, we gain a deeper appreciation for the ingenuity, cultural diversity, and interconnectedness of our prehistoric past.

The Future of Prehistoric Civilizations Research

As we journey through the ancient ruins and artifacts left behind by our prehistoric ancestors, we often find ourselves captivated by the mysteries and wonders of their civilizations. Prehistoric civilizations and societies have fascinated humans for centuries, and the study of these ancient cultures continues to evolve. We will explore the future of prehistoric civilizations research and the exciting developments that lie ahead.

One of the most innovative areas in prehistoric civilizations research is the use of advanced technologies. With the advent of cutting-edge techniques such as LiDAR (Light Detection and Ranging), archaeologists can now uncover hidden ruins and landscapes that were previously inaccessible. The use of drones and satellite imaging has also revolutionized the field, allowing researchers to map out vast areas and discover new archaeological sites. As technology continues to advance, we can expect even more groundbreaking discoveries in the years to come.

Another aspect that holds great promise for the future of prehistoric civilizations research is interdisciplinary collaboration. Archaeologists are increasingly working alongside experts from fields such as genetics, anthropology, and climatology, allowing for a comprehensive understanding of ancient cultures. By combining different disciplines, researchers can gain insights into aspects of prehistoric civilizations that were previously unseen. For example, DNA analysis can help reconstruct ancient populations and trace their migration patterns, shedding light on the origins of different civilizations.

Furthermore, the future of prehistoric civilizations research will be greatly influenced by the ongoing preservation and conservation efforts. As the threat of climate change looms, it is crucial to protect archaeological sites from natural disasters and human activities. Governments and organizations are increasingly recognizing the importance of safeguarding these invaluable remnants of our past. By investing in conservation efforts and sustainable practices, we can ensure that future generations will have the opportunity to explore and study prehistoric civilizations.

Lastly, the future of prehistoric civilizations research lies in the hands of passionate individuals who are dedicated to unraveling the mysteries of our ancestors. As more people become intrigued by the study of prehistoric civilizations, the field will continue to grow and flourish. Through continued education, public outreach programs, and the sharing of knowledge, we can inspire a new generation of archaeologists and researchers.

In conclusion, the future of prehistoric civilizations research is filled with exciting prospects. From technological advancements to interdisciplinary collaboration and conversation efforts, the field is poised for remarkable discoveries. As adults interested in prehistoric civilizations and societies, let us embrace these developments and look forward to a future where the secrets of our ancestors are unveiled, enriching our understanding of human history.

Chapter Twelve:

Walking in Their Footsteps: Understanding Our Ancestors

Lessons from Prehistoric Civilizations

In the vast tapestry of human history, prehistoric civilizations stand as the foundation of our modern societies. These ancient cultures, shrouded in mystery and intrigue, offer invaluable lessons that continue to resonate with us today. As we journey through the footsteps of our ancestors, we are granted a unique opportunity to understand the origins of our own existence and appreciate the wisdom of those who came before us.

One of the most significant lessons we can learn from prehistoric civilizations is the importance of community and collaboration. These ancient societies thrived on the principles of cooperation and mutual support. From the creation of intricate cave paintings to the construction of monumental structures like Stonehenge, it is evident that prehistoric humans recognized the power of collective effort. In a world often plagued by individualism and division, we can look to our ancestors for inspiration and strive to build stronger communities based on trust and unity.

Another valuable lesson we can glean from prehistoric civilizations is the deep connection between humans and nature. These ancient cultures lived in harmony with the natural world, recognizing the interdependence between humans and their environment. From their intimate knowledge of celestial movements to their profound understanding of agricultural cycles, prehistoric humans revered and respected nature. Today, as we face the consequences of environmental degradation, we can learn from our ancestors' reverence for the Earth and work towards sustainable practices that ensure a better future for generations to come.

Moreover, prehistoric civilizations teach us the importance of adaptability and resilience. These ancient cultures faced numerous challenges and hardships, yet they persevered and thrived. From the harsh conditions of the ice age to the constant threat of predators, prehistoric humans developed remarkable survival skills and innovative techniques. Their ability to adapt to changing circumstances and overcome adversity is a lesson that resonates with us in our modern world, where flexibility and resilience are essential qualities for success.

Lastly, prehistoric civilizations remind us of the inherent creativity and ingenuity of humanity. The exquisite cave paintings, intricate tools, and awe-inspiring architecture left behind by our ancestors are a testament to their incredible creativity. By studying and appreciating their artistic achievements, we can tap into our own creative potential and embrace the power of imagination.

In conclusion, the lessons from prehistoric civilizations are not confined to the annals of history; they continue to shape and inspire us today. Through the values of community, connection with nature, adaptability, and creativity, we can learn from our ancient ancestors and forge a better future. By embracing these lessons, we can honor the legacy of prehistoric civilizations and ensure their wisdom endures for generations to come.

CULTURAL HERITAGE AND
Preservation

In the vast tapestry of human history, prehistoric civilizations serve as the foundation upon which our modern societies have been built. These ancient cultures, with their fascinating rituals, innovative technologies, and awe-inspiring monuments, hold a wealth of knowledge and wisdom waiting to be explored. As adults with a keen interest in prehistoric civilizations and societies, we have the unique opportunity to delve into the footsteps of our ancestors and unravel the mysteries they left behind.

The preservation of cultural heritage is of utmost importance in our quest to understand and appreciate prehistoric civilizations. It is through the careful study and interpretation of artifacts, architecture, and ancient sites that we gain insight into the beliefs, values, and daily lives of our ancient predecessors. By preserving these remnants of the past, we ensure that their stories are not lost to time, allowing us to forge a deeper connection with our heritage.

One remarkable example of cultural preservation is the UNESCO World Heritage Sites, which encompass outstanding cultural and natural wonders from around the globe. These sites not only preserve the physical remains of prehistoric civilizations but also serve as reminders of our shared human history. From the towering pyramids of Egypt to the enigmatic stone circles of Stonehenge, these sites offer a glimpse into the remarkable achievements of our ancestors and provide a platform for continued research and understanding.

Furthermore, cultural heritage preservation extends beyond physical artifacts and sites. It encompasses the intangible aspects of prehistoric civilizations, such as their languages, myths, and oral traditions. Through the documentation and revitalization of these cultural practices, we can revive ancient languages, revive forgotten stories, and ensure the survival of unique cultural expressions.

As adults with a passion for prehistoric civilizations, we have a responsibility to contribute to the preservation and understanding of our cultural heritage. We can support archaeological research, visit museums and heritage sites, and educate ourselves and others about the significance of our ancient past. By doing so, we not only honor the achievements of our ancestors but also ensure that future generations can continue to explore and learn from the rich tapestry of human history.

In conclusion, through the preservation of physical artifacts, ancient sites, and intangible cultural practices, we can ensure that the stories and achievements of prehistoric civilizations are not lost to time. Let us embark on this journey together, honoring our ancestors and gaining a deeper appreciation for the rich tapestry of human history. We must understand the importance of preserving and understanding our cultural heritage, as it provides a gateway to our past and enriches our present.

THE RELEVANCE OF PREHISTORIC Civilizations to Modern Society

Prehistoric civilizations may seem like distant echoes from the past, but their relevance to modern society cannot be overstated. These ancient societies, with their unique cultures and ways of life, offer us valuable insights into our own existence and help us understand the trajectory of human development. We will delve into the significance of prehistoric civilizations and how they continue to shape our world today.

One of the most compelling reasons to study prehistoric civilizations is to gain a deeper understanding of human evolution. By examining their tools, art, and burial practices, we can trace the origins of our technological advancements, artistic expressions, and societal structures. These early civilizations laid the foundation for our modern world, and by studying their achievements and mistakes, we can learn valuable lessons for our own society.

Furthermore, prehistoric civilizations provide us with a sense of perspective and humility. They remind us that human history is not solely defined by the last few centuries but stretches back thousands of years. By appreciating the ingenuity and resilience of our ancestors, we can develop a greater appreciation for the complexities of our own society and the challenges we face.

Moreover, examining prehistoric civilizations can shed light on the interconnectedness of human cultures. Despite being geographically and temporally distant, these ancient societies often share striking similarities in their beliefs, practices, and social structures. By recognizing these commonalities, we can foster a sense of global unity and cultivate cross-cultural understanding in our increasingly interconnected world.

In addition, studying prehistoric civilizations can offer valuable insights into sustainable living and environmental stewardship. Many of these ancient societies had profound relationships with nature and lived in harmony with their surroundings. By learning from their sustainable practices, we can develop more eco-friendly approaches and address the pressing environmental issues facing our planet today.

Finally, exploring prehistoric civilizations can be an enriching and intellectually stimulating endeavor. It allows us to embark on a journey of discovery, piecing together the fragments of our collective past and connecting with our shared human heritage. By engaging with the mysteries and wonders of prehistoric civilizations, we can foster a sense of wonder and appreciation for the diversity and resilience of the human experience.

In conclusion, prehistoric civilizations hold immense relevance to modern society. They offer us insights into our own evolution, provide a sense of perspective, foster cross-cultural understanding, inspire sustainable living, and provide intellectual stimulation. By studying these ancient societies, we can better understand ourselves, our world, and the challenges and opportunities that lie ahead.

Don't miss out!

Visit the website below and you can sign up to receive emails whenever Linda Standridge publishes a new book. There's no charge and no obligation.

https://books2read.com/r/B-A-IMCBB-JXASC

BOOKS2READ

Connecting independent readers to independent writers.

About the Author

Linda Standridge is a small-town southern gal. She spends her days fantasizing about sexy aliens or simply writing about sexy aliens. When she isn't doing that she is spending time with her grandchildren and her children. She enjoys gardening and crocheting too. She promises she hasn't lost it entirely. She just loves talking about herself in the third person. She'd love to hear from ya'll.

Give her a shout-out at lindastandridgeauthor@gmail.com